DIGITAL MARKETING MASTERY

A Comprehensive Guide for Entrepreneurs"

BY

MAXEN FAISAL

TABLE OF CONTENTS

INTRODUCTION

CHAPTER 1
UNDERSTANDING THE LANDSCAPE OF
DIGITAL MARKETING,

CHAPTER 2
DEVELOPING A SUCCESSFUL DIGITAL
MARKETING PLAN.

CHAPTER 3.
UNDERSTANDING KEY DIGITAL MARKETING
CHANNELS IS

CHAPTER 4
ANALYTICS, TRACKING, AND OPTIMIZATION
ARE COVERED IN
IMPLEMENTING WEB ANALYTICS TOOLS

CHAPTER 5.
OPTIMIZING RETURN ON INVESTMENT (ROI)

CHAPTER 6
STAYING AHEAD OF THE DIGITAL MARKETING
CURVE.

CONCLUSION.
 BECOMING A DIGITAL MARKETING MASTER.

INTRODUCTION.

The significance of digital marketing cannot be overstated in the quickly changing business environment of today. Businesses of all sizes are realizing the enormous potential of digital channels to reach and engage their target audiences as technology continues to shape how we connect, communicate, and consume information. Digital marketing has developed into a crucial pillar of success in the contemporary business world, from social media platforms and search engines to email campaigns and online advertising.

Digital Marketing Mastery is a thorough manual created to equip business professionals, marketers, and entrepreneurs with the knowledge and abilities needed to successfully negotiate this ever-changing environment and become experts in the field of digital marketing.

This book will serve as your success road map, whether you're an experienced marketer looking to hone your techniques or a company owner eager to harness the power of digital channels.

In these pages, we'll delve into the complex world of digital marketing and examine the different plans, devices, and methods that produce results. But first, let's take a moment to understand why digital marketing is so important in today's business environment before we delve into the specifics.

A.
a description of the significance of digital marketing in the current business environment.

Digital marketing has completely changed how companies interact with their audiences and market their goods or services. Digital marketing, in contrast to traditional marketing strategies, provides unmatched reach, targeting options, and measurability. Businesses have an unprecedented opportunity to engage with their target customers at scale due to the billions of people who use social media platforms, the millions of searches made online every second, and the pervasiveness of email.

Digital marketing enables companies in previously unthinkable ways to increase customer loyalty, drive website traffic, and generate leads, and brand awareness. If startups and small businesses have a thorough understanding of digital marketing strategies and can make effective use of them, it levels the playing field and makes it possible for them to compete with established brands on a global scale.

B.
Introduce the idea of mastering digital marketing briefly.

Mastering digital marketing involves more than just sprinkling in a few tactics here and there. It includes a comprehensive understanding of the digital landscape, a strategic mindset, and the capacity to change with the dynamics of the online world. Understanding the fundamentals is only one part of becoming a master of digital marketing; other skills include keeping up with new trends, utilizing data-driven insights, and continuously fine-tuning strategies to get the best results.

In this book, we'll examine the fundamental ideas, ideal procedures, and practical tactics that will enable you to become an expert in digital marketing. This book will give you the information and resources required to confidently navigate the digital marketing landscape and experience outstanding success, from creating a solid foundation and a successful digital marketing strategy to mastering key channels and maximizing return on investment.

So let's start this transformational journey together, revealing the techniques of masterful digital marketing and laying the foundation for your company's success in the digital era.

CHAPTER 1

UNDERSTANDING THE LANDSCAPE OF DIGITAL MARKETING,

SECTION A

Having a thorough understanding of the digital marketing landscape is crucial for achieving digital marketing mastery. In addition to emphasizing the value of using a multi-channel strategy, this section will give you a thorough overview of the most important digital marketing channels.

Defining Key Digital Marketing Channels.
Digital marketing encompasses a diverse range of channels, each with its own special qualities and benefits. We will investigate the following important channels.

a. Social media: Social media platforms have completely changed the way that companies interact and connect with their target market. We'll examine well-known platforms like Facebook, Instagram, Twitter, and LinkedIn in-depth and go over tactics for making the most of them to promote brand awareness, strengthen client relationships, and increase website traffic.

b. Search engine optimization (SEO) is essential for increasing the visibility of your website in search engine results. In this lesson, we'll go over the fundamentals of SEO, such as keyword research, on-page optimization, and link building, to help you improve your website's organic rankings and draw in targeted traffic.

c. Email marketing is still one of the best ways to interact with customers and nurture leads, despite the emergence of newer channels. We'll talk about how crucial it is to develop an email list, create effective email campaigns, and use automation to send relevant messages to your audience.

discussing the significance of a multi-channel strategy.

While each digital marketing channel has its own advantages, it's imperative to use a multi-channel strategy to increase your reach and impact. We will examine the advantages of including various channels in your marketing strategy and examine how they can support and reinforce one another to produce a unified and powerful brand presence. Understanding the advantages and disadvantages of various channels will enable you to develop an integrated marketing strategy that amplifies your message across a variety of touchpoints.

SECTION B: Identifying Your Target Audience And Developing Buyer Personas.

You need to have a thorough understanding of your target market if you want to succeed in digital marketing. We'll walk you through the steps of identifying your target market and developing thorough buyer personas in this section.

Identifying Your Target Market.

We'll go over the significance of market segmentation and assist you in determining the particular demographic(s) that are most likely to be interested in your goods or services. You can learn a lot about the needs, preferences, and pain points of your audience by looking at demographic, psychographic, and behavioral factors.

Establishing Buyer Personas.

A fictionalized version of your ideal customers is provided by buyer personas. By examining their characteristics, objectives, difficulties, preferences, and purchasing patterns, we will lead you through the process of developing thorough buyer personas. Understanding your buyer personas will enable you to develop marketing messages, content, and offers that speak directly to their needs, thereby improving engagement and conversion rates.

SECTION C: Smart Digital Marketing Goal-setting Is Covered In

To direct your digital marketing efforts and assess your success, it is essential to set specific, quantifiable goals. In this section, we'll explain the idea of SMART goals and walk you through how to create concrete goals for your digital marketing campaigns.

SMART goal understanding.
We will describe the SMART framework— Specific, Measurable, Attainable, Relevant, and Time-bound—and provide examples of how it can be used in digital marketing. Setting objectives that fit these requirements will enable you to create precise benchmarks, monitor your progress, and make data-driven choices to improve your campaigns.

Choosing your digital marketing objectives.
Based on the knowledge we have gained from knowing your target audience, we will assist you in defining your digital marketing

objectives. Whether your objectives are to raise brand awareness, increase website traffic, create leads, or increase sales, we will offer advice on creating precise, doable goals that are consistent with your overarching business goals.

You can create a solid framework for developing your digital marketing strategies and tactics by laying a solid foundation in understanding the landscape of digital marketing, identifying your target audience, and setting SMART goals. We will examine each channel in more detail in the following chapters, giving you useful information and advice you can use to improve your knowledge of digital marketing.

CHAPTER 2

DEVELOPING A SUCCESSFUL DIGITAL MARKETING PLAN.

SECTION A: Conducting Competitive Analysis and Market Research.

Conducting extensive market research and competitive analysis is essential before beginning your digital marketing campaigns. In this section, we'll walk you through the process of learning crucial details about your target market and your competitors.

Knowing Who Your Target Market Is.

For a deeper understanding of your target market, we'll look at a variety of research techniques, such as surveys, interviews, and data analysis. You can spot opportunities and make adjustments to your marketing messages so that they are more effective with your audience by looking at variables like demographics, psychographics, behavior patterns, and preferences.

Investigating Your Rivals.

Understanding your competitors' strengths, weaknesses, and strategies is made possible by competitive analysis. We'll offer methods for assessing the websites, social media profiles, content, and marketing initiatives of rival companies. You can find gaps and create a distinctive value proposition by gaining insight into their positioning and strategies.

SECTION B: Creating Your USP (Unique Selling Proposition).

A strong Unique Selling Proposition (USP) is essential for differentiating your company in the crowded digital market and grabbing the attention of your target audience. The process of effectively defining and communicating your USP will be walked you through in this section.

Identifying Your Special Value.
We will work with you to pinpoint your distinctive advantages, differentiators, and value propositions. You will be able to explain what makes you different from your competitors and why customers should choose you by critically examining your products, services, customer experience, and brand positioning.

Making Your Unique Selling Proposition.
We'll walk you through the process of transforming your distinctive value into a compelling USP.
You can craft a compelling message that connects with your target audience and motivates them to act by concentrating on the

major advantages and results your customers can anticipate.

SECTION C.Building a Comprehensive Digital Marketing Plan,

A thorough digital marketing strategy serves as a road map, directing your work and ensuring consistency across all channels.
The process of creating a strategic and workable digital marketing plan will be demonstrated to you in this section.

Setting Goals and Key Performance Indicators (KPIs).
We will assist you in setting up quantifiable KPIs and coordinating your digital marketing objectives with your overall company goals. You can track your progress and make data-driven decisions to optimize your campaigns by

establishing specific goals and determining the metrics that matter most.

Finding Targeted Digital Marketing Channels.
We will investigate the most relevant and efficient digital marketing channels for reaching and engaging your target audience based on that group. You can allocate resources wisely and increase your ROI by choosing the appropriate channels.

Outlining the tactics and strategies.
We'll delve into a variety of digital marketing techniques and strategies, such as social media marketing, search engine optimization (SEO), email marketing, content marketing, and paid advertising. We'll go over how each channel can be used to accomplish particular goals and offer implementation advice.

SECTION D: Formulating a Content Marketing Plan.

A potent tool for drawing in, retaining, and converting your target audience is content marketing. We will walk you through the process of developing a content marketing strategy that is in line with your overall digital marketing objectives in this section.

Realizing The Significance Of Content Marketing.

We'll look at the importance of content marketing in the digital sphere and how it can help you establish your brand's authority, generate traffic, and nurture leads.
You will be inspired to produce worthwhile and pertinent content for your audience once you are aware of the advantages of content marketing.

Setting Goals for Your Content Marketing.

In accordance with your target market, buyer personas, and overarching business objectives, we will assist you in defining your content marketing objectives.

We'll show you how to establish specific, quantifiable content marketing goals, whether they're aimed at increasing brand awareness, educating potential customers, or generating conversions.

creating a plan for the creation and distribution of content.

You will be guided through the process of making a content calendar, selecting content topics, formats, and distribution channels. We'll go over the best techniques for producing interesting and shareable content, optimizing it for search engines, and using a variety of distribution channels, like social media, email newsletters, and guest blogging.

You will position yourself for success in the constantly changing digital environment by developing a successful digital marketing strategy that incorporates market research, a unique selling proposition, a thorough digital marketing plan, and a content marketing strategy. We will examine each strategy in greater detail and offer practical advice in the following chapters to help you hone your mastery of digital marketing.

CHAPTER 3.

UNDERSTANDING KEY DIGITAL MARKETING CHANNELS IS

Search engine optimization (SEO) is covered in Section A.

Any effective digital marketing strategy must include search engine optimization (SEO). On-page and off-page optimization strategies will be the main topics of this section's investigation into the ins and outs of SEO.

Techniques for on-page optimization.
We'll delve into the foundational components of on-page optimization, such as keyword research, meta tag improvement, producing high-quality and pertinent content, enhancing website speed and user experience, and putting appropriate URL structures in place. Your website will appear more prominently in search engine results and draw organic traffic if the on-page components are optimized.

Techniques for Off-Page Optimization.

Building authority and generating backlinks to your website are both greatly aided by off-page optimization. We will talk about efficient link-building tactics like outreach, guest blogging, and working with influencers. We will also discuss how managing your online reputation, social signals, and user-generated content can improve the off-page SEO of your website.

Social Media Marketing Section B.

Social media platforms provide businesses with unmatched opportunities to engage with their audience and strengthen their brand presence. You will receive instruction on how to master social media marketing in this section.

The Best Social Media Platforms for Your Business.
We'll look at well-known social media sites like Facebook, Instagram, Twitter, LinkedIn, and YouTube and help you decide which ones best suit your target market and professional objectives. You can create a customized social media strategy by being aware of the distinctive qualities of each platform.

Creating Content That Is Shareable and Engaging.
The most effective methods for producing engaging social media content, including photos, videos, and blog posts, will be covered. We'll go into detail about how to write captivating captions, use hashtags wisely, and boost audience interaction. We will also look

into how to use user-generated content and promote brand advocacy on social media.

utilizing advertising on social media.
Your reach and ability to target particular demographics can both be greatly improved by social media advertising. We'll discuss a variety of social media advertising strategies, such as sponsored posts, targeted ads, and retargeting campaigns. We'll go over how to create marketing campaigns, specify audience targeting criteria, improve ad performance, and calculate ROI.

Part C: Email Marketing.

One of the best strategies for nurturing leads, developing connections, and increasing conversions is email marketing. In this section, we'll examine the essential components of effective email marketing.

Building a Successful Email List.

We'll walk you through the steps of creating a top-notch email list, including techniques for gathering email addresses, segmenting your audience, and adhering to email marketing laws. The significance of permission-based marketing will be emphasized, and we'll offer advice on how to increase your subscriber base.

Designing Effective Email Campaigns.
We will go over the key elements of an effective email campaign, such as developing attention-grabbing subject lines, personalizing content, utilizing persuasive copywriting strategies, and including powerful calls to action. We will also look at various email campaign types, including newsletters, advertising emails, and drip campaigns that are automated.

Workflows for email marketing automation.
Your email marketing efforts can be greatly streamlined by automation, which also increases effectiveness. We will introduce you to email marketing automation tools and walk you through setting up automated workflows, like

welcome emails, abandoned cart reminders, and customer re-engagement campaigns. We'll also go over how crucial it is to monitor email metrics and carry out A/B testing to improve email performance.

Pay-Per-Click (PPC) Advertising is covered in Section D.

Pay-Per-Click (PPC) advertising enables you to display ads on search engine results pages and other online platforms to attract targeted traffic to your website. We'll look at the PPC advertising basics in this section.

Understanding the PPC Advertising Foundations.
We will give an overview of PPC advertising, including how it functions, various ad networks (like Google Ads and Bing Ads), and ad formats. To ensure you have a strong foundation for building successful PPC campaigns, we will thoroughly explain the

concept of keywords, bidding strategies, and quality score.

Making Successful Advertising Campaigns.

We will lead you through the steps of developing persuading ad copy, choosing pertinent keywords, and optimizing landing pages for higher conversion rates. To optimize your ad performance and accomplish your campaign goals, we will go over best practices for ad targeting, ad extensions, and ad testing.

Increasing ROI with PPC Campaign Optimization.
For PPC advertising to provide a favorable return on investment (ROI), ongoing monitoring and optimization are required. In order to optimize your PPC campaigns, we'll look at methods for reviewing campaign data, pinpointing problem areas, and coming to informed decisions. In order to maximize your ROI and the efficiency of your PPC advertising efforts, we'll also talk about conversion

tracking, remarketing, and bid management strategies.

You can drive targeted traffic, engage your audience, and accomplish your digital marketing objectives by mastering important digital marketing channels like SEO, social media marketing, email marketing, and PPC advertising. Your understanding of digital marketing will be further improved as we delve deeper into advanced strategies and tactics within each channel in the following chapters.

CHAPTER 4

ANALYTICS, TRACKING, AND OPTIMIZATION ARE COVERED IN IMPLEMENTING WEB ANALYTICS TOOLS,

SECTION A

It is essential to use web analytics tools, which offer insightful data on user behavior and website performance, in order to evaluate the success of your digital marketing initiatives. We'll look at how to use web analytics tools effectively in this section.

The Best Web Analytics Tool Selection.
We'll talk about well-known web analytics programs like Hotjar, Adobe Analytics, and Google Analytics. We will assist you in

comprehending their advantages, drawbacks, and features so you can choose the tool that most closely matches your company's requirements.

Tracking Web Analytics Configuration.
Setting up web analytics tracking on your website is something we'll walk you through step-by-step. We'll go over installing tracking codes, setting up objectives and events, and monitoring online purchase activity. You can learn a lot about how well your digital marketing is performing by precisely tracking user interactions and conversions.

SECTION B: Examining Key Performance Indicators (KPIs) for the Success of Digital Marketing.

To evaluate the success of your digital marketing campaigns and make data-driven decisions, it is critical to analyze key performance indicators (KPIs). We will examine the main KPIs in this section that you should track and evaluate.

Choosing Useful KPIs.

We'll go over a variety of KPIs that are pertinent to various digital marketing channels and goals. These could include things like website traffic, conversion rates, click-through rates, bounce rates, social media engagement, email open rates, and revenue made. We'll work with you to find the KPIs that support your objectives and offer useful information.

Making Informed Decisions Based on Data Interpretation.

In this section, we'll examine methods for deciphering and analyzing data gathered by web analytics tools. To better comprehend your audience and the effectiveness of your campaigns, we will talk about data visualization, segmentation, and benchmarking. Utilizing these insights will enable you to optimize your digital marketing strategies and make wise decisions.

SECTION C:Conversion rate optimization and split testing are covered in

Split testing, also referred to as A/B testing, is a potent method for streamlining your digital marketing initiatives and raising conversion rates. We will examine split testing and conversion rate optimization in this section.

Recognizing split testing.

We will define the idea of split testing and discuss its importance in digital marketing. We will walk you through the steps involved in designing and putting split tests into action, including choosing variables, coming up with test iterations, and gathering data. You can fine-tune your marketing strategies and determine which parts of your campaigns are most successful by conducting split tests.

CRO, or conversion rate optimization.

We will investigate methods for raising conversion rates, including enhancing landing pages, call-to-action buttons, forms, and checkout procedures. The best methods for conducting user experience (UX) audits, heatmaps, and user testing to locate conversion bottlenecks and enhance the user experience will be covered.

SECTION D: Continual Improvement And Change Adaptation.

Since the world of digital marketing is constantly changing, it's critical to constantly enhance and modify your tactics if you want to keep up.
We'll talk about the value of adapting to change and continuous improvement in this section.

tracking updates and trends in the industry.

We'll look at methods for keeping abreast of the most recent business trends, algorithm updates, and technological developments.
We will go over how important it is to follow industry blogs, go to conferences, and engage in online communities in order to stay informed and adjust your strategies as necessary.

taking a growth mindset to heart.
We will stress the significance of adopting a growth mindset in digital marketing. We will talk about the importance of trying new things, picking yourself up after mistakes, and adopting a data-driven strategy. You can maintain your position as a leader in the field of digital marketing by consistently looking for ways to get better and being adaptable.

You will have the framework in place to optimize your digital marketing efforts and experience greater success by putting web analytics tools into use, analyzing KPIs, running split tests, and continuously improving and adapting your strategies. We'll examine more sophisticated methods and tactics in the following chapters to help you become an even better expert in digital marketing.

CHAPTER 5.

OPTIMIZING RETURN ON INVESTMENT (ROI)

Budgeting and resource allocation for digital marketing are covered in Section A.

To get the most return on your investment (ROI) from digital marketing, it's essential to manage your budget and resources well. We will look at resource allocation and budgeting strategies in this section.

determining a budget for digital marketing.
We will go over the elements to take into account when deciding on a digital marketing budget, such as business objectives, sector benchmarks, and available resources. Based on their potential impact and alignment with your objectives, we will walk you through the

process of distributing your budget among various digital marketing channels and tactics.

enhancing resource allocation.

We'll look at methods for maximizing resource allocation within your digital marketing team or company. We will go over how to evaluate skills and expertise, assign duties, and use automation or outsourcing tools to work as efficiently and effectively as possible.

Measurement and analysis of ROI is covered in Section B.

To evaluate the effectiveness and profitability of your digital marketing campaigns, measuring and analyzing ROI is crucial. We will examine the techniques and resources for accurately measuring and analyzing ROI in this section.

Making ROI Metrics Specific.

We will help you identify the appropriate ROI metrics for your digital marketing campaigns, such as return on ad spend (ROAS), customer lifetime value (CLV), cost per acquisition (CPA), and revenue generated. We will discuss the importance of aligning these metrics with your business goals and tracking them consistently.

Analyzing ROI Data.

We will explore techniques for analyzing ROI data collected from various digital marketing channels and tools. We will discuss methods for attributing conversions to specific marketing activities, conducting attribution modeling, and evaluating the profitability of different campaigns. By analyzing ROI data, you can identify high-performing campaigns, optimize underperforming ones, and make data-driven decisions.

Section C: Scaling Successful Campaigns and Strategies.

Once you identify successful campaigns and strategies, scaling them effectively is key to maximizing ROI. In this section, we will discuss strategies for scaling your digital marketing efforts.

Replicating Successful Campaigns.
We will explore techniques for replicating successful campaigns across different channels, target segments, or geographic locations. We will discuss adapting campaign elements, such as messaging, creative assets, and targeting parameters, to ensure consistent performance and scalability.

Leveraging Automation and Technology.
We will discuss the role of automation and technology in scaling digital marketing efforts. We will explore marketing automation tools, customer relationship management (CRM) systems, and data management platforms (DMPs) to streamline processes, improve personalization, and increase efficiency.

Section D: Identifying and Mitigating Digital Marketing Risks.

Digital marketing involves inherent risks, and it is essential to identify and mitigate them to safeguard your ROI. In this section, we will discuss strategies for identifying and mitigating digital marketing risks.

Conducting Risk Assessments.
We will guide you through the process of conducting risk assessments for your digital marketing campaigns and strategies. We will discuss identifying potential risks, such as ad fraud, data breaches, algorithm changes, and reputational risks. We will explore techniques for evaluating the likelihood and impact of these risks and developing mitigation plans.

Staying Agile and Adaptable.
We will emphasize the importance of staying agile and adaptable in the face of evolving digital marketing risks. We will discuss techniques for monitoring industry trends,

staying informed about regulatory changes, and developing contingency plans. By being proactive and agile, you can minimize the impact of potential risks on your ROI.

By effectively budgeting, measuring and analyzing ROI, scaling successful campaigns and strategies, and mitigating digital marketing risks, you will be well-equipped to maximize your return on investment in the digital marketing realm. In the subsequent chapters, we will explore advanced tactics and emerging trends to further enhance your digital marketing mastery.

CHAPTER 6

STAYING AHEAD OF THE DIGITAL MARKETING CURVE.

Section A: Keeping up with Industry Trends and Best Practices.

Staying informed about the latest industry trends and best practices is crucial to maintaining a competitive edge in digital marketing. In this section, we will explore strategies for keeping up with industry trends and staying ahead of the curve.

Following Industry Publications and Influencers.

We will discuss the importance of following reputable industry publications, blogs, and thought leaders in the field of digital marketing. By staying up-to-date with the latest news, insights, and case studies, you can gain valuable knowledge and stay ahead of emerging trends.

Engaging in Professional Communities.

We will explore the benefits of actively participating in professional communities, such as online forums, social media groups, and industry-specific events. Engaging with like-minded professionals allows you to exchange ideas, share experiences, and learn from others in the digital marketing community.

Section B: Embracing Emerging Technologies and Platforms.

The digital marketing landscape is constantly evolving, with new technologies and platforms emerging regularly. In this section, we will discuss the importance of embracing emerging technologies and platforms to stay ahead.

Monitoring Emerging Technologies.
We will explore emerging technologies such as artificial intelligence (AI), virtual reality (VR), augmented reality (AR), chatbots, and voice search. We will discuss their potential applications in digital marketing and how to stay informed about their advancements.

Experimenting with New Platforms.
We will discuss the significance of experimenting with new platforms, such as emerging social media networks, video-sharing platforms, or messaging apps. By being an early adopter, you can gain a competitive advantage and reach new audiences.

Section C: Leveraging Data-Driven Insights for Strategic Decision-Making.

Data-driven insights play a vital role in shaping successful digital marketing strategies. In this section, we will explore techniques for leveraging data-driven insights to make informed and strategic decisions.

Collecting and Analyzing Data.
We will discuss the importance of collecting and analyzing data from various digital marketing channels, such as web analytics, social media analytics, and customer relationship management (CRM) systems. We will explore techniques for data collection, data integration, and data analysis to gain actionable insights.

Applying Insights to Strategy.
We will explore how to translate data-driven insights into strategic decisions. We will discuss techniques for segmenting audiences, personalizing content, optimizing customer journeys, and refining marketing campaigns based on data insights. By applying data-driven insights, you can enhance the effectiveness and ROI of your digital marketing efforts.

Section D: Developing a Culture of Continuous Learning and Innovation.

Digital marketing is a dynamic field that requires a culture of continuous learning and innovation. In this section, we will discuss the importance of fostering a culture of continuous learning and innovation within your organization.

Encouraging Professional Development.
We will explore strategies for encouraging ongoing professional development within your digital marketing team. This may include providing training opportunities, supporting certifications, and organizing knowledge-sharing sessions. By investing in continuous learning, you can equip your team with the skills and knowledge needed to stay ahead.

Promoting Experimentation and Innovation.

We will discuss the value of promoting experimentation and innovation within your organization. We will explore techniques for fostering a creative and innovative environment, such as encouraging brainstorming sessions, allowing for risk-taking, and recognizing and rewarding innovative ideas. By embracing experimentation and innovation, you can uncover new strategies and approaches to digital marketing.

By actively keeping up with industry trends and best practices, embracing emerging technologies and platforms, leveraging data-driven insights, and developing a culture of continuous learning and innovation, you will position yourself as a digital marketing leader. In the subsequent chapters, we will explore advanced tactics, emerging trends, and real-world case studies to further enhance your digital marketing mastery.

CONCLUSION.

BECOMING A DIGITAL MARKETING MASTER.

In this book, we embarked on a journey to unlock the secrets of digital marketing mastery. We explored the importance of digital marketing in today's business landscape and introduced the concept of digital marketing mastery. Throughout the chapters, we covered various key aspects of digital marketing, providing you with the knowledge and strategies to excel in this dynamic field. As we conclude this book, let's recap the key points covered, encourage you to apply the knowledge gained, and inspire you to become a digital marketing master.

A. Recap of Key Points Covered.

Throughout this book, we delved into the essentials of digital marketing, providing a comprehensive understanding of its various components. We started by building a strong foundation, understanding the digital marketing landscape, defining target audiences, and setting SMART goals. We then explored crafting winning digital marketing strategies, including market research, defining unique selling propositions, developing comprehensive plans, and creating compelling content.

Moving forward, we discussed mastering key digital marketing channels such as search engine optimization (SEO), social media marketing, email marketing, and pay-per-click (PPC) advertising. We explored optimization techniques, engagement strategies, list building, and effective ad campaign creation. We then explored tracking, analytics, and optimization, including implementing web analytics tools, analyzing key performance indicators (KPIs), split testing, and continuous improvement.

Furthermore, we discussed maximizing return on investment (ROI) by effectively budgeting, measuring and analyzing ROI, scaling successful campaigns, and mitigating digital marketing risks. Lastly, we emphasized the importance of staying ahead of the digital marketing curve by keeping up with industry trends, embracing emerging technologies, leveraging data-driven insights, and fostering a culture of continuous learning and innovation.

B. Encouragement to Apply the Knowledge Gained and Take Action.

Knowledge without action is merely potential. Now that you have gained valuable insights and strategies in digital marketing, it is crucial to apply this knowledge and take action. Digital marketing is a practical discipline that requires experimentation, adaptation, and continuous improvement. It is through action that you will truly master the art of digital marketing.

Take the knowledge you have acquired and put it into practice. Implement the strategies, techniques, and best practices covered in this book. Track your results, analyze data, and make informed decisions based on insights. Don't be afraid to experiment, take calculated risks, and learn from both successes and failures. Remember, digital marketing is an ever-evolving field, and staying proactive and adaptive will be key to your success.

C. Inspiring Readers to Become Digital Marketing Masters.

As we conclude this book, our final message is one of inspiration. Becoming a digital marketing master is not just about acquiring knowledge; it is about embracing a mindset of continuous learning, innovation, and excellence. The journey of mastery is a lifelong pursuit, filled with challenges, opportunities, and immense rewards.

By becoming a digital marketing master, you have the power to transform businesses, connect with audiences, and drive meaningful results. You have the ability to navigate the digital landscape with confidence and create impactful strategies that resonate with your target audience. Embrace your role as a digital marketing leader and inspire others with your knowledge, skills, and passion.

Remember, the mastery of digital marketing is not confined to the pages of this book. It is an ongoing process that requires dedication, perseverance, and a commitment to lifelong learning. Stay curious, stay hungry for knowledge, and continue exploring new frontiers in digital marketing.

Congratulations on embarking on this journey towards digital marketing mastery. Now, it is up to you to take what you have learned and make a profound impact in the digital realm. The future of digital marketing awaits your innovation and expertise. Go forth and become a digital marketing master!

www.ingramcontent.com/pod-product-compliance
Lightning Source LLC
Chambersburg PA
CBHW062258290526
45794CB00006B/2603